PANZERWRECKS 26 INDEX

Vehicles

Identified Locations

Identified German Units

panzerwrecks.com

After Kampfgruppe Peiper captured Stoumont on the morning of 19 December 1944, 2./SS-Panzer-Regiment 1 set out to pursue the enemy and reached Stoumont Station in the Amblève valley, 4 km west of the town, in the afternoon. There, four Panthers were knocked out, including Panther '211'. The tank was assembled by M.A.N. in September 1944 and had the chassis number 121047. The tactical number was originally '212', but was subsequently changed to '211', evidence of which can be seen here. This is only on the left side; the right side did not have this change, so it was probably a mistake originally.

E.Montfort

Panther '211' was one of a limited number fitted with resilient steel-tyred wheels, originally designed for the Panther II. The camouflage pattern is clearly discernible in both photos. The tank probably suffered an internal explosion, as the GI is peering in through a hatchless commander's cupola, and there is blackening on the bottom of the gun mantlet. **1x Panzerwrecks, 1x T.Haasler**

Panther Ausf.G
2./SS-Pz.Rgt.1, 1.SS-Panzer-Division
Stoumont Station, Belgium

212

RODNA

This page: The same family as page 1, but this wider view shows Stoumont Station and a wrecked German ambulance in the background. As Panther '211' approached Stoumont Station on 19 December 1944, it was fired on by an M4 tank from 740th Tank Battalion at a range of about 200 yards, ricochetting off the bottom of the gun mantlet, setting off the stowed ammunition. The Panther was subsequently pushed off the road to its resting place between the road and railway tracks.

E.Montfort

Opposite: A photograph taken by the US Army Judge Advocate General's Corps (JAG) in 1946. The N633 road is in the background, along with the wreck of Panther '232', which became stuck in the ditch on the side of the road and later bulldozed to clear the road. This view shows that Panther '211's idler wheel has taken a hit from an armour-piercing round which would have broken the track. By this time, the hub cap on the drive sprocket has been removed. The M.A.N. September 1944 camouflage pattern is very clear to see.

Ellis Collection via Darren Neely

Opposite: In the foreground is Panther '232' on its side in the roadside ditch. In the background, '211' has started to be cut up by scrap merchants. A third Panther, number '215' was knocked out a little further up the road.
3x Panzerwrecks, 1x Stefan De Meyer Collection

This page: Poor quality photos showing Panther '211' with a wrecked German ambulance in the background.
  1x Stefan De Meyer Collection, 1x J.Tomkinson

Opposite, this and next page: Located in Square Crépin, Rochefort, this Jagdpanther was featured in *Panzerwrecks 16*. The vehicle, from s.H.Pz.Jg.Abt.559 and attached to Panzer-Lehr-Division, was knocked out on 23 December by a hit to the right side. The unit diary mentions two or three Jagdpanthers were lost in the defence of Rochefort.

Opposite top: The Jagdpanther was originally knocked out on the N35, but later moved to Square Crépin.

Next page: Scrap merchants have begun cutting the vehicle into manageable pieces, providing a unique view of the gun and its mount fixed to the floor, as well as the exposed engine. Pieces of cut-up armour are scattered across the foreground.
3x Stefan De Meyer Collection, 4x Panzerwrecks

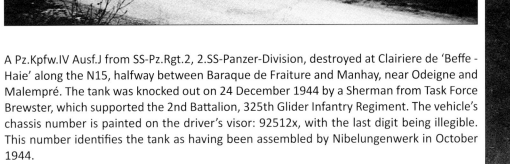

A Pz.Kpfw.IV Ausf.J from SS-Pz.Rgt.2, 2.SS-Panzer-Division, destroyed at Clairiere de 'Beffe - Haie' along the N15, halfway between Baraque de Fraiture and Manhay, near Odeigne and Malempré. The tank was knocked out on 24 December 1944 by a Sherman from Task Force Brewster, which supported the 2nd Battalion, 325th Glider Infantry Regiment. The vehicle's chassis number is painted on the driver's visor: 92512x, with the last digit being illegible. This number identifies the tank as having been assembled by Nibelungenwerk in October 1944.

4x Stefan De Meyer Collection

Cpl. Peter Piar, Lt. John Perkins and Pfc. Calvin DuPre of the US 291st Combat Engineers remove a booby trap from a Sturmgeschütz III of Kampfgruppe Y, Panzer-Brigade 150 in Géromont on 15 January 1945. Despite accounts of five Sturmgeschütze being camouflaged as fantasy US vehicles, we have only found photographic evidence of thisGéromont vehicle.

Our working theory is that it was abandoned on the N32 road, as seen here, with the muzzle brake still in place. All other photos show it after being pushed into the adjacent field, where it rolled some way down the hill.

NARA

Two photos from *ETO Technical Intelligence Report No.171 dated 8 March 1945*. The photographs are now missing from the report at the US National Archives.

SUBJECT: *German Assault Gun Disguised as U.S. Army Vehicle.*

Observations by: Capt. L.M. Darrow and Lt. E.M. Whitaker, Ord. Tech. Intell. Team No.1.

1. GENERAL:

A German self-propelled assault gun, 7.5cm Sturmgeschutz [sic] 40 Model G, Sd.Kfz.142, which was disguised to represent a U.S. combat vehicle was knocked out near MALMEDY, Belgium, in January 1945. The type of disguise and method of modification, which had apparently been applied in some advance enemy shop, were for the purpose of confusing and deceiving our forces in the 'breakthrough' of December, 1944.

2. DETAILED MODIFICATIONS:

*a. **Painting:** The vehicle was painted dark green with two white stars on each side and one white star on the front and rear of the vehicle. In addition, the vehicle was stencilled in white on the front and back with markings for vehicle 'C 5' of the '81st Regiment, 5th Armored Division'.*

*b. **Suspension:** The type of suspension was concealed by three 2mm (5/64 inch) thick steel sheets fastened by twelve 1/2 x 1 inch machine bolts to the mudguards on each of the vehicle. The overlapping vertical joint between each of the sheets was secured by three of the same bolts. These steel skirts extended to within approximately eight inches of the ground. Indications are that these skirts were readily deformed when the vehicle traversed uneven terrain.*

*c. **False Engine Compartment Cover:** A false cover of 2mm (5/64 inch) thick steel sheeting extended from the upper rear edge of the fighting compartment to the upper rear edge of the engine compartment. It was bolted to a framework consisting of 25/64 inch x 25/32 inch x 9/64 inch angle iron reinforced at the corners by 1 3/8 inch x 1 3/8 inch x 13/64 inch angle iron. The welded joints of the framework and the welded joints attaching the framework to the hull exhibited poor workmanship. The bulged appearance of the false cover in the photographs results from the explosion of an H.E. shell in the engine compartment.*

*d. **No muzzle brake was found with the vehicle.** It is not known whether the muzzle brake had been removed as part of the deception, or after the vehicle was disabled. Modification of the recoil cylinder would be necessary if the gun was to be fired without the muzzle brake.*

*e. **Camouflage Net:** A U.S. Army type camouflage net (coarse mesh) was found partially draped over the vehicle. The Germans customarily use a net with a finer mesh.*

1x Stefan De Meyer Collection, 1x S.Zaloga

The Géromont Sturmgeschütz in the summer of 1945 or 1946. Quite what US vehicle the Germans were trying to imitate is anyone's guess. Operation Greif planned for Panzer-Brigade 150 to operate behind enemy lines. When it became clear that the brigade could not infiltrate the American lines undetected, it was ordered to deploy as a regular combat unit. On 21 December 1944, the brigade attacked American positions in the Malmedy area but failed.

2x MLG

It seems the Sturmgeschütze were not used during the brigade's attack on 21 December 1944 because they could not fight effectively at night. They were supposed to come in as backup if the fighting went on into daylight. However, there is no sign they were involved at all that day, so we do not know when or how the Sturmgeschütz was lost. Given that it was rigged with booby traps, it likely broke down and could not be recovered.

MLG

RODNA

5△81△

Page 16: Good close-ups of this vehicle are difficult to find. The camouflage net mentioned in the technical intelligence report can be clearly seen in this photo, probably taken in the winter of 1945. **This page:** The camouflage net has gone. The sheet metal 'skirts' over the tracks were fixed using metal straps bolted to the trackguard, and can see one has been ripped off. The sliding gunsight cover is out place, possibly indicating an explosion in the fighting compartment. Readers will also note that only the 15 January photo on page 12 shows the 'Rundumfeuer' M.G. mount, making us think that the Americans removed it. The fake markings are for the US 5th Armored Division, 81st Tank Battalion.

1x AMC, 1x Panzerwrecks

The wreck some time later. The US markings on the bow and superstructure side have started to fade, although the paint used to cover the original German camouflage has lasted well. By now, track, wheels and smaller items have been removed. The white writing on the bow probably identifies the scrap merchant who has the rights to around twenty-plus tonnes of recyclable steel in this vehicle.

Stefan De Meyer Collection

A Sturmgeschütz III Ausf.G on the outskirts of Hargimont, on the Marloie road. On the night of 24/25 December, the first elements of Pz.Rgt.33, 9.Panzer-Division, arrived in the Hargimont area to relieve the 2.Panzer-Division. While the exact arrival date of 1./Pz.Rgt.33 in Hargimont is unknown, it is documented that the company was deployed in the area until the general retreat began, having lost only 4 of its original 14 Sturmgeschütze by that time. Consequently, it is likely that this Sturmgeschütz belonged to 1./Pz.Rgt.33. The method of attaching the 'Schürzen' is unusual, as is their bend at the trackguard. An illegible name has been painted on the bow armour. **1x J.Tomkinson, 1x Stefan De Meyer Collection**

More views of the Sturmgeschütz in Hargimont, displaying its tactical number '111' and the brackets used to mount the 'Schürzen' on the sides of the fighting compartment. According to the photo caption, the man perched atop the vehicle is Arthur Romarin. Souvenir hunters have removed two armoured hubcaps from the roadwheels. Interestingly, the vehicle originally had two 'Balkenkreuze' on the rear armour, although these are not visible in these photographs. **2x Stefan De Meyer Collection**

A vignette for modellers. Two M.I.A.G assembled Sturmgeschütze from 5./ or 6./Pz.Rgt.3, 2.Panzer-Division, were knocked out on the N4 road in Hollogne: one outside a house and the other in a vegetable patch. The vehicle outside the house features a coaxial M.G. in the box mantlet and lacks 'Zimmerit'. Despite a thorough search, we have not been able to identify the location of this house or vegetable patch.

3x Stefan De Meyer Collection

Opposite: A clearer view of the Sturmgeschütz in the vegetable patch reveals that it has 'Zimmerit', unlike the other vehicle. The damage to the trackguard might be concealing a hit.

On the evening of 22 December, forward elements of 2.Panzer-Division reached the road junction at Hollogne, 2 kilometres east of Marche. There, the spearhead encountered stiff American resistance and was unable to capture the town by surprise. At least two Sturmgeschütze from 5./ or 6./Pz.Rgt.3 were destroyed before the Germans withdrew. The 2.Panzer-Division subsequently attempted to bypass Marche to the west via Harsin and Hargimont.

J.Tomkinson

This page: Elsewhere in Hollogne, a third Sturmgeschütz was destroyed. In the bottom photo, the number '62' can be seen stencilled in white on the side of the superstructure. Given this tactical number, it was likely from 6./Pz.Rgt.3.

1x Stefan De Meyer Collection, 1x USAHEC

The (Alkett-assembled) Sturmgeschütz from page 25 was photographed some time after the war. By this time, the building in the background had its stone facade rendered, and the windows replaced and renovated. The Sturmgeschütz is missing several parts of its running gear, including a drive sprocket, two roadwheels, an idler, return rollers, and sections of track. Additionally, the 30mm extra armour on the driver's front plate has been removed. **Stefan De Meyer Collection**

A M.I.A.G. assembled Sturmgeschütz III Ausf.G pushed down a hill in Luxembourg. The photo on the left, taken by Tony Krier in 1945, shows the brushed-on whitewash paint job. The photo on the right was taken some time later, after the gun barrel and bolted-on armour plates had been removed. The number '792' might be part of the chassis number. The edge of the road in the top right of the photo illustrates how steep the hill is.

1x VDL, 1x Panzerwrecks

A late-production Hummel from SS-Pz.Art.Rgt.1, 1.SS-Panzer-Division, has been pushed off the road near the Trois-Ponts - Coo railway line. It was among a group of vehicles attempting to join up with Kampfgruppe Peiper in La Gleize on 20 December 1944, but destroyed by Task Force Lovelady. **1x Panzerwrecks, 1x C.Barney, 1x NARA**

The photo above was taken after the accessible parts of the running gear, and armoured cover over the driver's area, had been removed. Readers of Panzerwrecks will be familiar with the fact that when Hummels were hit, the rear often suffered catastrophic damage due to the ammunition being protected by only 15mm of armour plate.

1x Stefan De Meyer Collection, 1x C.Barney

This page: Hscha. Frauscher, commander of the 3 Zug, 4./SS-Pz.Rgt.2, 2.SS-Panzer-Division, was leading the company's advance on Manhay via Odeigne on 24 December. He was in Panther '431', followed by Hstuf. Pohl, the company commander, in Panther '402', Oscha. Barkmann, the company troop commander, in Panther '401', then the rest of the company. Near Odeigne, Frauscher's tank was badly damaged by American fire, prompting him to take over another tank in his platoon. Unbeknownst to him, Barkmann in his Panther had taken the lead. Still believing he was leading the attack, Frauscher entered Manhay about an hour after leaving Odeigne. At the crossroads, Capt. Malcolm of the 40th Tank Battalion, 7th Armored Division, spotted the leading German tank and knocked it out. The tank following Frauscher's Panther returned fire and destroyed the Sherman. Once again, Frauscher emerged unharmed and commandeered his third tank of the night. **Top left:** A grainy photo of the Panther before being pushed off the road. **Opposite:** The Panther, now missing its muzzle brake, showing chicken wire on the turret side.

1x Stefan De Meyer Collection, 3x NARA

Opposite: Views of the Panther and its surroundings, including Captain Malcolm's Sherman. **This page:** The Panther has 'Zimmerit' on the turret but not on the hull, and the first two digits of the chassis number are visible on the gun travel lock. Next to the radio operator's hatch is a hole in the roof armour, cause unknown. It is presumed that the cut-away armour from the Panther's turret was repurposed for a US tank.

1x Panzerwrecks, 4x Stefan De Meyer Collection

The I./Pz.Rgt.3, 2.Panzer-Division, was attacked on its right flank by American forces and fighter bombers on 23 and 24 December in the area west and northwest of Marche. This picture was taken 500 metres northeast of Forzée, on the road to Baillonville, near the junction with the N29 to Givet. The Panther, an Ausf.G, has often been mistakenly identified as belonging to Pz.Lehr.Rgt.130. However, this is unlikely. When the Panzer-Lehr-Division advanced northeast from the Rochefort area on 24 and 25 December to support 2.Panzer-Division, it aimed to capture Humain and Buissonville. Although Humain was briefly captured, the division failed to secure Buissonville. **NARA**

The Forzée Panther was hit by armour-piercing shells on the turret side, with some visible at the bottom and one notable hit near the top. The severity of the damage suggests that the engine bay likely caught fire, as evidenced by the blackening of the rear plate.

3x Stefan De Meyer Collection, 1x Panzerwrecks

Opposite: A Flakpanzer IV 'Wirbelwind' destroyed in Marnach, Luxembourg. The gun mount appears to be intact, but the barrels are missing, along with several hatches, return rollers, and an idler wheel. Wirbelwinds were assembled on rebuilt Pz.Kpfw.IV Ausf.G and H chassis; this one an Ausf.G with no 'Zimmerit'. Of particular note is the armour plug on the side behind the radio operator's position; the original location of the radio antenna.

Stefan De Meyer Collection

This page: A Wirbelwind in Baraque de Fraiture, probably from SS-Pz.Rgt.2, 2.SS-Panzer-Division, which had four combat-ready Wirbelwinde on 15 December 1944 and 1 January 1945. The new crew appears to be Belgian Police. Despite the poor quality of the photo, it is evident that the vehicle still retains its gun barrels and tracks. The purpose of the small protrusions around the turret is not known. The glacis plate is covered with ammunition magazines for the 2cm Flakvierling 38, indicating that the vehicle may have been abandoned in relatively intact condition.

Stefan De Meyer Collection

The armoured vanguard of Kampfgruppe Peiper had already lost two Panthers in a minefield west of Losheim and a Pz.Kpfw. IV in another minefield near Merscheid on the night of 16/17 December 1944. On the morning of 17 December, it received orders to lead the attack on Büllingen. At the fork in the road on the southern edge of Büllingen, the leading Pz.Kpfw.IV, commanded by Schf. Horst Rempel and numbered '725', was knocked out by a bazooka.

The Pz.Kpfw.IV of Ostuf. Werner Sternebeck, the leader of the vanguard, was following. He reported: *"A few hundred metres south of the entrance to Büllingen, in a place where it was difficult to see, the fourth Panzer directly in front of me was destroyed by close combat weapons. There were no survivors."*

Later, Ustuf. Arndt Fischer passed this spot in his Panther: *"In the Büllingen area, Oberscharführer Rempel's tank was hit, and Rempel was killed. I saw him lying dead on his tank when I passed it."* The soldier who knocked out the Pz.IV with the bazooka was Grant Yager of the 924th US Artillery Battalion. He was captured shortly after. Fortunately, the Germans did not identify him as the man who had recently destroyed a German tank.

The vehicle is an Ausf.J, from 7./SS-Pz. Rgt.1, 1.SS-Panzer-Division. The lower photo clearly shows the tank's distinctive 'Licht und Schatten' (light and shadow) camouflage pattern.

1x T.Haasler, 1x Panzerwrecks

What look to be Belgian Police pose for a photo on a Pz.Kpfw.IV Ausf.J in the Losheim – Honsfeld – Hünningen area, and likely from SS-Pz.Rgt.12, 12.SS-Panzer-Division. The tank is missing the track and idler wheel. The rear 'Schürzen' panels are missing, revealing the small rectangular bracket fixed to the rear of the turret bin. **Panzerwrecks**

This mittlerer Funkpanzerwagen (Sd.Kfz.251/3) photographed in Baraque de Fraiture appears to have been destroyed by a shot through the driver's visor. As is often the case, the outer roadwheels and front wheel have been pilfered. The 'Balkenkreuz' on the vehicle is styled in a manner consistent with 2.SS-Panzer-Division, suggesting that it likely belonged to SS-Pz.Aufkl.Abt.2 or I./SS-Pz.Gren.Rgt.3. The heart insignia has been seen on a number of 2.SS-Pz.Div. vehicles. Spare track links were stowed in the lockers, as visible in the photo. The radio rack on top of the fighting compartment identifies the vehicle as a m.Fu.Pz.Wg. (Sd.Kfz.251/3) rather than the standard APC. **Stefan De Meyer Collection**

American soldiers examine an abandoned mittlerer Schützenpanzerwagen (Sd.Kfz.251) in the snow. The 'Balkenkreuz' style suggests the vehicle belonged to 2.SS-Panzer-Division, although the reason for the divisional insignia being painted on the side remains unclear.

The tactical number '4410' identifies it as belonging to 4./SS-Pz.Gren.Rgt.3. The vehicle is positioned adjacent to the railway line.

Panzerwrecks

While the Panthers destroyed at Stoumont Station on 19 December 1944 receive the most attention (see pages 1-7), 1.SS-Panzer-Division also lost a Sd.Kfz.251 from III./SS-Pz.Gren. Rgt.2. Although both photos are of poor quality, the main image reveals that a 'Panzerschild' for the M.G.42 has been fitted at the rear. Above the driver's compartment, there appears to be a mount for a s.M.G. The vehicle is notably missing its entire front section and most of the rear compartment. **1x Panzerwrecks, 1x Stefan De Meyer Collection**

This Sd.Kfz.251 has suffered extensive damage, with most of the armoured rear compartment completely blown away. What remains includes only the front driver's section and the rear wall. The vehicle has a faint tactical sign next to the licence plate. A tow cable has been fixed in the starter port rather than the tow hooks. **Panzerwrecks**

Left: An American MP poses next to a Sd.Kfz.251 with an Army licence plate, tactical number '02', probably from 2.Panzer-Division. The vehicle is missing its outer roadwheels.
Right: This schwerer Panzerspähwagen (7.5cm) (Sd.Kfz.233) of St./Pz.Aufkl.Abt.2,

2.Panzer-Division, was captured on 25 December in the Foy-Notre-Dame area and moved to a vehicle collection point northeast of Celles, where the picture was taken. The tactical number was '1152', as seen on page 83 of *Panzerwrecks 16*. **2x Panzerwrecks**

A m.S.P.W. (Sd.Kfz.251/1) in Mierchamps, 1945, with its outer road wheels, front road wheel, and engine access covers removed. The neat hole in the 8mm side armour of the engine compartment might have knocked the vehicle out. Remains of a whitewash over the sprayed camouflage pattern are still visible, and a fresh white block has been painted on the nose, presumably to make the wreck more obvious to drivers at night. It has not been possible to identify the unit.

Panzerwrecks

A mittlerer Krankenpanzerwagen (Sd.Kfz.251/8) abandoned next to the church in Neffe. Note its light colour, probably a coat of whitewash, and the enormous red crosses on its side. The mittlerer Krankenpanzerwagen was not fitted with an M.G. shield because it did not have a machine gun, only a single M.P.40.

NARA

On the morning of 26 December 1944, the advance guard of the 116.Panzer-Division, comprising Pz.Aufkl.Abt.116, 1./Pz.Jg.Abt.228 and II./Pz.Art.Rgt.146, was to attack from the area southwest of Verdenne to the northeast and first take Hill 326 west of Verdenne. Then it was to push into the west part of the town held by elements of the 84th US Inf Div and then establish contact with Kampfgruppe Bayer, which was surrounded to the northeast of Verdenne. The force managed to take Hill 326 in the morning against stiff resistance, but the attack on Verdenne was thwarted by fire from American anti-tank and artillery guns. By early afternoon, Hill 326 had to be abandoned. **Stefan De Meyer Collection**

These photos show an Sturmgeschütz III Ausf.G from 1./Pz.Jg.Abt.228 and a mittlerer Krankenpanzerwagen (Sd.Kfz.251/8) southwest of Verdenne in the area of Hill 326. Verdenne church can be seen in the background of this photo. Both vehicles were destroyed by artillery fire or the anti-tank guns on the edge of the town. The tactical number on the m.Kr.Wg. is puzzling, as the first number refers to a company, for example 7./Pz.Gren. Rgt.60 or 7./Pz.Rgt.16. However, m.Kr.Wg. belonged to the 'Stab' and were not an integral part of the companies, so we cannot positively identify the unit.

Stefan De Meyer Collection

A head-on view of the Sturmgeschütz and ambulance. The StuG had spare tracks on hooks fitted to the front of the superstructure. The m.Kr.Wg. has an angle-iron bumper welded to the bow armour, a feature seen on several of 116.Pz.Div.'s Sd.Kfz.251s. One or two m.Kr. Wg. (Sd.Kfz.251/8) were issued to the Stabs-Kompanie (Headquarters Company) of most armoured units.

Stefan De Meyer Collection

Taken some time later, after a door and the outer road wheels have been removed, the right side of the m.Kr.Wg. (Sd.Kfz.251/8) is revealed. Below the right-hand rear door is a foldable step, a feature unique to the m.Kr.Wg. Being slightly better exposed than the other side views, we can see the large red cross painted on the side. It looks like there is a hole next to the co-driver's position.

AMC

This page: Not a great photo, but a rare one. A m.S.P.W. (2cm) (Sd.Kfz.251/17) photographed near Noville, probably from I./Pz.Gren.Rgt.2, 2.Panzer-Division. The front armour section is missing, along with the radiator and most of the contents of the engine compartment. The rear has been shortened by an explosion. **Stefan De Meyer Collection**

Opposite: Pvt. Edward Hoyt of Coalinga, CA, examines a US-made M2 machine gun on a mittlerer Schützenpanzerwagen (Sd.Kfz.251/1) Ausf.C in Marcourt on 13 January 1945. Likely users were I./Pz.Gren.Rgt.60 or Führer-Begleit-Brigade. In the background is the River Ourthe. **NARA**

The reinforced Pz.Aufkl.Abt.116 arrived in the Beffé area on 21 December and was initially ordered to attack northwards via Dochamps, but it faced resistance to the north and northwest of the town. The battalion then moved east via Lamorménil towards Amonines. After capturing Lamorménil, it advanced towards Amonines. At 21:00, Pz.Aufkl.Abt.116 reached the edge of the forest 1 kilometre southeast of Amonines. However, the spearhead encountered heavy defensive fire and suffered significant losses, halting the attack. On the left is a le.S.P.W. (Sd.Kfz.250/1) Ausf.B, note its squashed front fender. On the right is an Sd.Kfz.250 Ausf.A armed with a 2cm Kw.K. Further down the road is a le.Fu.Pz.Wg. (Sd.Kfz.250/3), and beyond that is another Sd.Kfz.250/1.

NARA

This photo was taken on 4 January 1945, after the wrecks were pushed into the field next to the building. The scalloped edge design of the gun shield for the 2cm Kw.K.-armed Sd.Kfz.250 is interesting, as is the fact that the armoured body has separated from the chassis. There are two US tanks either side of the house on the right in the background. **NARA**

This is the le.S.P.W. (Sd.kfz.250) from the previous page, now missing a front wheel and an engine access cover. Interestingly, the tactical number '246' has been painted over the original 'Balkenkreuz', and a fresh one hand-painted between the stowage lockers.

Another example of this is on page 59 of *Panzerwrecks 21*, and is from the same unit: Pz.Aufkl.Abt.116.

SV/HW/TH

A leichter Funkpanzerwagen (Sd.Kfz.250/3) or leichter Beobachtungspanzerwagen (Sd. Kfz.250/5) has overturned between Odeigne and Malempré. Unlike the vehicle opposite, it has no tactical number, just a large Balkenkreuz painted on the side armour. Given the location, the halftrack is probably from the 2.SS-Panzer-Division. An interesting detail is the 'Antennenfuß aus Stahlblech' fitted to the extra antenna. This metal sprung mount was introduced in late 1944 to save rubber. **Stefan De Meyer Collection**

An M8 Light Armored Car used by the Germans and knocked out or abandoned in Neffe (see *Panzerwrecks 16* for more examples). Very distinctive 'Balkenkreuze' have been painted between the driver's and radio operator's hatches, on the glacis plate, turret side, and hull side. **Stefan De Meyer Collection**

Two Sturmgeschütze from Kampfgruppe Maucke (Pz.Abt.115, 15.Panzergrenadier-Division) were destroyed as they crossed the frozen ground towards Hemroulle on 25 December 1944. The Sturmgeschütz in the foreground is missing the commander's cupola. **TTM**

The German High Command ordered the 26.Volksgrenadier-Division to destroy the Bastogne pocket by 25 December 1944. The division planned concentric attacks from the east, south, and west, focusing on the area west of Bastogne. The terrain between Champs and Mande St. Etienne was ideal for tank attacks.

Kampfgruppe Maucke, composed of Pz.Gren.Rgt.115, Pz.Abt.115 (both 15.Pz.Gren.Div.), Gren.Rgt.77, and Aufkl.Abt.26 (both 26.V.G.Div.) led the attack. I./Pz.Gren.Rgt.115 would attack in the centre on the right, parallel to the main Marche-Bastogne road, with 11 tanks from 2./ and 3./Pz.Abt.115. III./Pz.Gren.Rgt.115 would attack on the left, supported by just three anti-tank guns. Gren.Rgt.77 would take the left flank, advancing via Champs to Hemroulle. Aufkl.Abt.26 would take the right flank, advancing from Mande St. Etienne to Isle la Hesse. The reserve was II./Pz.Gren.Rgt.115.

The attack was to begin at 03:00 and Bastogne was to be captured by 09:00. Oberst Maucke's regiment had set out from Euskirchen on 20 December, reaching Trois Monts by midnight on 24 December, leaving no time for deployment or reconnaissance.

The regiment prepared to attack at 02:30. I./Pz.Gren.Rgt.115 crossed the line at Flamierge at 03:00, with most of the grenadiers riding on tanks. The 3rd Battalion followed at 03:30

At 4:05, the vanguard reported Flamisoul clear of the enemy. Both battalions made good progress, and the enemy withdrew. At 06:00, Gren.Rgt.77 attacked Champs from Rouette, leading to heavy fighting. By 08:00, I./ and III./Pz.Gren.Rgt.115 reported stiff enemy resistance 2.5 km west of Bastogne. The 3rd Battalion reported flanking fire from Heights 514, 505 and Hemroulle. The battalion turned north, attacked Height 514, occupied it but got stuck under heavy enemy fire south of Hemroulle.

The attack faltered because the 1st Battalion was south of the Champs-Hemroulle road, just 2.5 km west of Bastogne, having run into the 327th Glider Infantry Regiment. The attacking tanks split and attacked Champs and Hemroulle but failed because all of Pz.Abt.115's tanks had been knocked out. This accounted for 11 tanks, not 17-18 as some American sources claim. Photos show 3 Pz.Kpfw.IVs and 6 Sturmgeschütze. Divisional reports indicate the loss of 6 Sturmgeschütze and 8 Pz.Kpfw.IVs up to 31 December 1944, including losses on 25 December and the following days.

Contrary to some sources, Panzerjägers from Pz.Jg.Abt.33 were not engaged on 25 December, but supported II./Pz.Gren.Rgt.115 that evening and were deployed on 26 December.

2x NARA

A front view of this Tiger I was featured in Darren Neely's *Forgotten Archives 1*. The only unit equipped with the Tiger I during the Ardennes Offensive was 4./s.H.Pz.Abt.506. Like this vehicle, many of the unit's Tigers were hybrids; this particular one has resilient steel wheels on an early model (without 'Zimmerit' and with a drum cupola). The vehicle appears to have been destroyed by its crew, as evidenced by the blown-out turret roof, sagging torsion bars, and a displaced turret. Close inspection reveals that the turret originally had smoke dischargers welded to its sides and that a penetration in the turret side (below the vision port) has been welded shut. **Panzerwrecks**

Another view of the 4./s.H.Pz.Abt.506 Tiger from pages 2 and 3 of *Panzerwrecks 16*, in Rodershausen, Luxembourg. Part of its tactical number, a '3', is visible on the turret side, the rest is covered by spare track links. The photo was taken in the spring or summer of 1945, and by this time a number of the outer roadwheels have been pilfered. With most of the 'Schürzen' gone, we can see how the sprayed camouflage pattern stops abruptly. The Tiger's tracks are worn smooth, although we can see 'Eisgreifer' (ice cleats) were fitted. These improved traction in snow and ice and, looking at this vehicle, were fitted to every fifth track link.

Panzerwrecks

This Tiger I was shown on pages 38 and 39 of *Panzerwrecks 16*. The tank, from 4./s.H.Pz. Abt.506, was destroyed attacking Oberwampach on 17/18 January 1945 as part of Kampfgruppe Gutmann. Like the Tigers on the previous pages, it is a hybrid with a mix of features: the old 'drum' cupola, no 'Zimmerit', but with resilient steel wheels. Like the Tiger opposite, it has 'Eisgreifer' fitted, visible above the idler wheel.

Stefan De Meyer Collection

65

We think this Tiger is from s.H.Pz.Abt.506. The photo opposite only tells part of the story: that the Tiger was crossing a field when US gunners targeted it, a shot ricocheting from the rear of the turret side - likely blowing off the spare tracks. The vertical lines visible in the curved section of the turret side are part of the manufacturing process. This page shows that another AP round hit the glacis plate, leaving a scar. A hit (or maybe two) in the sponson has probably cooked-off the stowed ammunition, blowing the sponson out and revealing just how thick the front armour actually was. The concrete added around the commander's cupola is an interesting addition. **1x T.Haasler, 1x Panzerwrecks**

This page: Two Flakwagen vehicles were destroyed near Lodomez, Belgium, on 18 December by a P-47 Thunderbolt from the US 506th Fighter Squadron dropping a 500 pound bomb. Both were from le.Fla.Stu.Abt.84, which was attached to Kampfgruppe Peiper just days before the start of the offensive. On the left is a 3.7cm Flak 36 auf Selbstfahrlafette (Daimler-Benz L4500A), while on the right is a Sfl. auf m.Zgkw.5t (Sd.Kfz.6/2) that was towing a Sd.Ah.57 (1 Achs) für Zubehör und Munition für 3.7cm Flak (Sfl). The top photo graphically illustrates the 85° elevation of the 3.7cm Flak 36.

2x NARA

Opposite: The same two Flakwagen some time later. The close-ups of the 3.7cm Flak 36 auf Selbstfahrlafette (Daimler-Benz L4500A) show that it suffered a catastrophic explosion. Nearby, a Schwimmwagen has slipped into the bomb crater.

3x Stefan De Meyer Collection

69

Opposite: The wreckage of two Nebelkraftwagen Sd.Kfz.11/1 or 11/4 and a Nebelwerfer in Tarchamps, probably from SS-Werfer-Abteilung 1. Note the ammunition racks behind the driving compartment; the Sd.Kfz.11/1 could hold 20x 10cm rounds, whereas the Sd.Kfz.11/4 could be outfitted for 28x 10cm rounds, 24x 15cm rounds, or 18x 21cm rounds.
This page: The halftracks photographed by a local some time later, after the useful items have been removed.

1x Panzerwrecks, 1x NACHF

A schwerer Wehrmachtsschlepper (s.W.S.) mit Pritschenaufbau, which according to the caption in the lower photo, was lost in Bihain, although the church spire in the top photo does not match what we see today. The s.W.S. was carrying an ammunition load, probably for an 8.8cm Pak gun.

1x R.Petrovich, 1x 823rd TD Bn via Darren Neely

Another destroyed schwerer Wehrmachtsschlepper mit Pritschenaufbau, pictured by the same US Army photographer, who photographed the Tiger on page 62, probably in Luxembourg. Parts of the load-bed have been blown away, and the front wheels are missing. Although covered in snow, the vehicle does not appear to have a camouflage paint scheme. The s.W.S. was a slow vehicle, with a top speed of just over 27 km/h (17 mph), but with significant towing power and cross country ability. **Panzerwrecks**

A smashed and overturned Jeep, a wrecked and overturned Sd.Kfz.251 and a snow-covered Pz.Kpfw.IV on Rue de Beausaint in La Roche-en-Ardenne. It is difficult to see, but the Panzer has been short-tracked, by whom, we don't know. The location now has a house on it. La Roche-en-Ardenne was liberated by the British 51st (Highland) Infantry Division on 11 January 1945.

2x Stefan De Meyer Collection

The La Roche-en-Ardenne Panzer IV was not a regular tank but a Befehlspanzer (command tank), as indicated by the armoured 'pot' on the rear for an extra radio antenna and the plugged coaxial M.G. opening. While we tend to think of the Germans using their latest vehicles in the Battle of the Bulge, this Befehlswagen is a rebuilt Ausf.G, featuring a driver's side vision port and 'Zimmerit' coating. The photo on the right shows its tactical number 'I01' indicates a Stabs Kompanie, probably I./Pz.Rgt.33, 9.Panzer-Division.

1x Panzerwrecks, 1x Stefan De Meyer Collection

The Befehlswagen was later moved up the road. It had spare track links on the driver's front plate, although only the retaining hooks remain. The lower photo shows the vehicle after scrap men began dissecting the wreck, starting with the back end, gun barrel, and commander's cupola.

2x Stefan De Meyer Collection

On 22 December 1944, s.H.Pz.Jg.Abt.560 made one last attack in the dark from Büllingen towards Domaine Bütgenbach. The aim was to engage American infantry in a small forest to the right of the road. Olt. Kröninger's Panzer IV/70(V) (commander of the 3rd Company) led the attack. To approach the forest, the company commander ordered the tank to turn into the meadow on the right of the road. However, it quickly became apparent that the snow-covered meadow was swampy. The tank became bogged down and was unable to move. A Jagdpanther commanded by Hptm. Wewers (commander of the 1st Company) was hastily summoned by radio to assist, but it was unable to tow the Panzer IV/70(V) free. The Jagdpanther even risked getting stuck itself.

The rescue attempt alerted the Americans, and artillery fire steadily increased. During the fighting, the Panzer IV/70(V) was hit several times and had to be abandoned. Meanwhile, a vehicle commander, Wöhlert, had also moved his Jagdpanther '131' into the meadow near the Reissbach, and it suffered the same fate as Kröninger. In a further attempt to rescue Wöhlert's vehicle, Wewers had his Jagdpanther '101' move into the meadow and also got stuck. While standing in the hatch, he was fatally wounded by a rifle bullet. Wewers' crew were also killed when bailing out, and the crew of Wöhlert's tank went missing. The German attack collapsed, and the remaining vehicles withdrew.

NARA

On 23 December 1944, commander Traut received orders to use his Jagdpanther '102' to pull Wöhlert's tank out of the meadow by the Reissbach on the night of 24 December. The rescue operation began at nightfall, but in the darkness Traut's tank moved past the accident site. The commander realised his mistake at the last moment and immediately ordered the driver to turn sharply to the right. At this point, the embankment leading into the meadow was 3-4 metres high, and the tank slipped down the slope, coming to a stop in the mud of the Reissbach. This meant that a third Jagdpanther was stuck in the meadow. With no help expected, it was finally abandoned on the night of 25 December. **AMC**

This page: A Belgian soldier (?) in the hatch of Jagdpanther '131', with '101' behind. An internal explosion has blown all but one of the hatches from the roof and blown out the driver's periscope. The hull of this Jagdpanther was manufactured for two periscopes, but only one was fitted, the other being blanked off with a 15mm section of armour plate. Small loops have been welded to the front of the roof plate and gun mantlet to fix camouflage materials.

AMC

Opposite: The tool brackets have been removed from the side of '131', and the track has been removed from the drive sprocket. In the background, '101's roof plate has been unseated by an internal explosion.

Stefan De Meyer Collection

Opposite: The tactical numbers of Jagdpanther '102' in the foreground, and '131' behind are visible. **This page:** An extremely rare colour photograph of the scene. The red oxide basecoat is clear to see, with patches of Dunkelgelb RAL 7028 on top. Over this is a light spray of Olivgrün RAL 6003. Note how the patterns differ between '102' in the foreground and '101' on the left, and that the camouflage pattern extends to the lower hull side. The tactical number was painted in black with a white outline.

1x Stefan De Meyer Collection, 1x Rueben S. Horst

Opposite: Jagdpanther '102'. Like '131', it has wire loops welded to the glacis plate and side, and wire has been threaded through them. **This page:** Jagdpanther '101' also has wire loops on the front plate.

2x Stefan De Meyer Collection

Jagdpanther '134' from 1./s.H.Pz.Jg.Abt.560 was knocked out while attacking along the Büllingen - Domaine Bütgenbach road on 20 December 1944. Nearby were a selection of s.H.Pz.Jg.Abt.560 and 12.SS-Pz.Div. vehicles. **Inset opposite:** The Jagdpanther's gun barrel was 'shortened' later. **This page:** Photos of the roof of the Jagdpanther are uncommon. It is interesting to note that the 80mm thick front plate has cracked. The gun cleaning rod tube has been relocated from the hull side to the rear of the engine deck. Like the vehicles on the previous pages, camouflage loops have been welded to the top of the side plate.

1x NARA, 2x USAHEC

Taken in brighter sunshine, these photos show the camouflage pattern on the side. The overturned vehicle next to the Jagdpanther in the top left photo is a Pz.Beob.Wg.IV from SS-Pz.Art.Rgt.12, tactical number 'B2'. See page 66 of *Panzerwrecks 4* for another photo.

3x T.Haasler

A well known photo showing a Pz.Kpfw.IV Ausf.J from 7. or 8./Pz.Rgt.3 and Panther Ausf.G from 1./Pz.Rgt.3, 2.Panzer-Division. Both tanks were destroyed near Noville on 19 or 20 December 1944, when 2.Panzer-Division attacked Task Force Desobry in the village. On 20 December, the task force was reinforced by a battalion from the 502nd Parachute Infantry Regiment, which tried to restore the situation by attacking in the early afternoon. However, this counterattack ran into a German attack, and both sides stalled. By 17:00, the last defenders had left Noville, and 2.Panzer-Division was able to continue its advance west in force. **NARA**

This page: Lesser-known photos of the Noville Panzers. In addition to losing its left track, the Pz.Kpfw.IV has two penetrations on the side of the fighting compartment and one that has gone through the turret 'Schürze' to penetrate the turret side. The tank features extended hull towing points and a swivelling commander's cupola. Meanwhile, the Panther has at least two holes in the hull side and small-arms scars on the turret.

2x J.Tomkinson, 1x Panzerwrecks

Opposite: The Panther has a series of AP hits on the glacis plate and a penetration at the junction of the glacis and lower bow armour. The Pz.Kpfw.IV's hull appears to have a 'spotted' camouflage pattern, which looks different from the turret.

4x Stefan De Meyer Collection

Panther '115' from SS-Pz.Rgt.1, 1.SS-Panzer-Division was knocked out as it approached the bridge over the River Amblève in Stavelot on 18 December. **Opposite top left:** The Panther in its original position was a hazard to road users. **Opposite, other photos:** It seems a push to the rear side was all that was needed to get the Panther off the road. **This page:** A great view over Stavelot. The large building to the left of the posing soldier is Stavelot Abbey.

2x Panzerwrecks, 3x Stefan De Meyer Collection

Most of the Panther's crew were wounded, and remained in Stavelot, but the commander, Uscha. Richartz, boarded another tank. Fire has blackened the gun mantlet. The object in the foreground is the radio rack.

Panzerwrecks

94

Taken from down the hill, looking up to the road, these views show the location of the 'Balkenkreuz' on the hull side; this identifies it as being assembled by Daimler-Benz.

1x Panzerwrecks, 2x Stefan De Meyer Collection

Tiger '332', from s.SS-Pz.Abt.501, was abandoned after breaking down on the side of the N33 at Coo on 18 December 1944. It was subsequently recovered by the 463rd Ordnance Evacuation Company using an M19 tractor, two M32 ARVs, and an M1A1 wrecker. After stopping at Stavelot on the 27th, the convoy reached Spa on 28 December, where it was left at the station. Fast forward to February 1945, and Ordnance Technical Inspection Team 1 (OTIT-1) examined the Tiger before it was transported to Antwerp on a captured German heavy trailer for eventual shipment to the USA.

USAHEC

A GI provides a size comparison. The Tiger was assembled by Henschel (as was standard for all Tigers) on 11 September 1944, with Fahrgestellnummer 280243. Initially issued to s.Pz. Abt.509, it was later transferred to s.SS-Pz.Abt.501.

USAHEC

This rear view shows the 80mm thickness of the hull and turret side armour. The tow cable snaking behind exhaust and through the tow shackle is from the right side. **USAHEC**

The Americans brought up an M4A3 Medium Tank as a comparison. As we can see here, the height and length were similar, but the Tiger was much wider; the difference in track width being particularly notable.

USAHEC

This page: The Tiger remained at Spa Station until February, when it was inspected by OTIT-1. The tank was sent to the United States for further inspection and was displayed at Aberdeen Proving Ground for 40 years before being transferred to the US Army Armor School in Kentucky in 1991. It is now on display at the National Armor and Cavalry Collection at Ft. Moore, Georgia.

USAHEC

Opposite: Photographed by OTIT-1, the turret has been traversed 90° to provide a view through the rear escape hatch. Inside the hatch is a sheet metal guard designed to protect the stowed ammunition from spalling caused by hits on the turret side. On the left is one of the ammunition racks, while the opened loader's hatch, visible at the top right, shows the details of its locking mechanism.

USAHEC

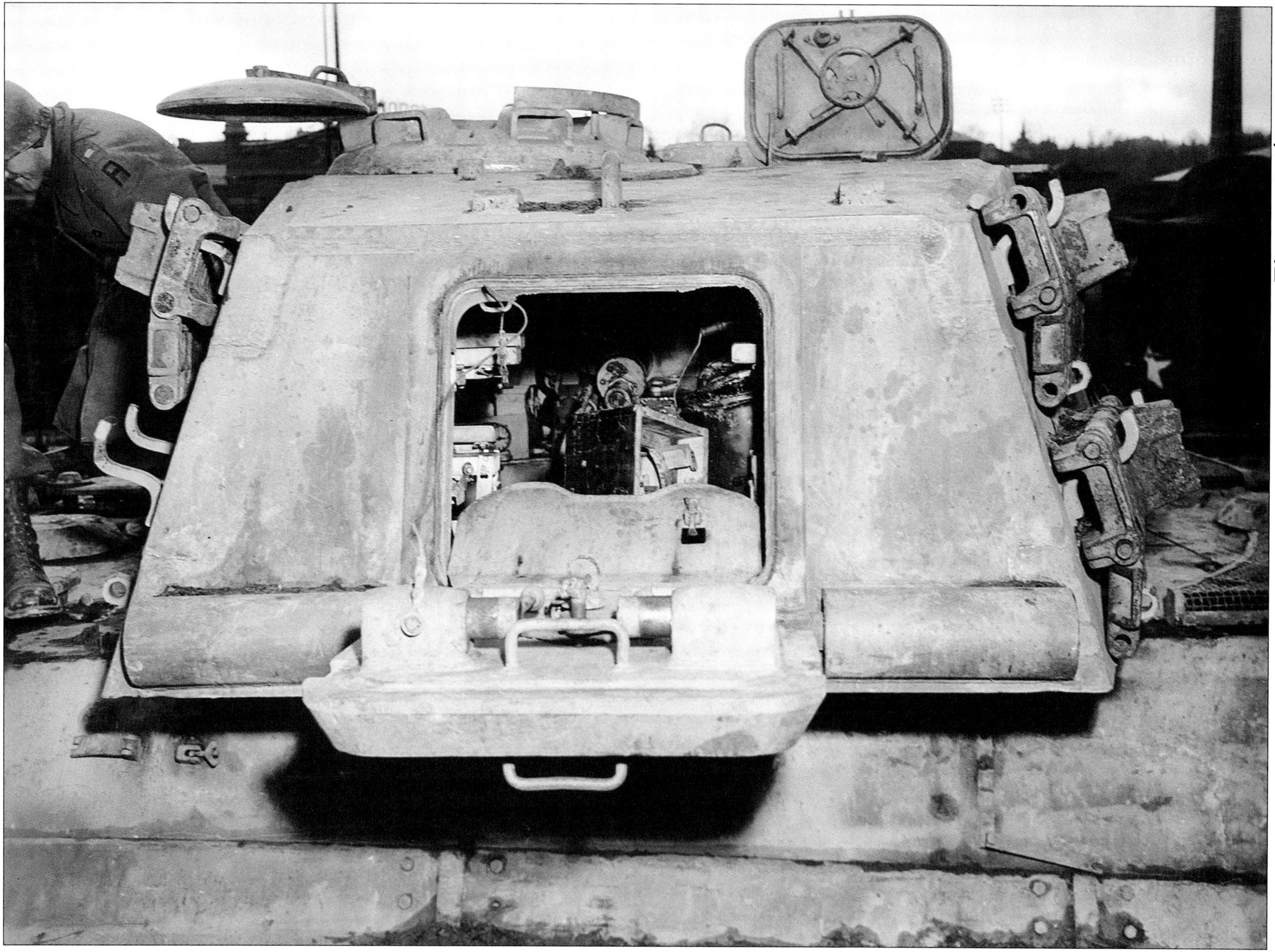

A close-up of the commander's cupola. This type, introduced in August 1944, was bolted to the turret roof, whereas the earlier version was welded. The design incorporated three rain channels, visible as grooves. The two small-diameter tubes inside the anti-aircraft ring were designed to accommodate a rain guard, a device not commonly seen in use. **USAHEC**

Seated in front of the commander, was the gunner. The dial-like device is an azimuth indicator, used to show the traverse of the turret. To its right is the T.Z.F.9d gunsight, which is missing the eyepiece. Below this is the traverse handwheel, while the black button above it is the emergency firing switch.

USAHEC

Looking down at the gunner's position, we see his seat and the turret traverse handwheel. The elevation handwheel is on the right, slightly beneath the gun. The bracket behind is the commander's footrest.

USAHEC

Left: The loader's position with M.G.34 mount and its spent casing chute. **Above:** The loader had an auxiliary traverse handwheel, visible here. The box above is the gun safety switch. **Opposite:** The left-hand ammunition racks in the turret bustle. A roller for loading the ammunition can be seen in the stowed position at the bottom left. **3x USAHEC**

Opposite: A Pz.Kpfw.IV Ausf.J in deep snow in Bihain. The turret has been dislodged, moving it forward. A name starting with 'Er' has been painted on the gun barrel. If the Bihain location is correct, the tank will be from 5./ or 6./SS-Pz.Rgt.9, 9.SS-Panzer-Division.

Panzerwrecks

This page: Close-up photos of this Pz.Kpfw.IV Ausf.J, destroyed in Marnach, were shown in *Panzerwrecks 1*. The destruction of the hull and turret are consistent with the crew setting demolition charges. The Panzer was from 7./ or 8./Pz.Rgt.3, 2.Panzer-Division and destroyed around 17 December 1944.

Stefan De Meyer Collection

A Pz.Kpfw.IV Ausf.J of 7. or 8./Pz.Rgt.3, 2.Panzer-Division lost during the division's withdrawal in January 1945 near Villers-sur-Lesse. Note the divisional 'Trident' insignia on the driver's front plate. The turret roof has been blown out making the gun depress much further than usual and unseating the commander's cupola.

AMC

This Flakpanzer IV 'Möbelwagen', destroyed near Sibret, would have been a large target against the skyline. It is shown here after the war, with nearly every wheel gone. It has single 25mm plate armoured sides, one of which has dropped down to the ground. Its 'Licht und Schatten' camouflage scheme is visible on the fold-down sides and hull. Only two Möbelwagen-equipped units were in the area: Pz.Abt.115 with two Möbelwagen, none of which were lost between 14 December 1944 and 10 February 1945; Pz.L.Rgt.130, which had six Flakpanzers (Möbelwagen and Wirbelwind), of which one was lost during the offensive. **Stefan De Meyer Collection**

More wreckage at Sibret. This Jagdpanzer 38 is interesting as it has a mix of features not often seen. It has the later driver's periscope and a 'Flammenvernichter' exhaust muffler, all features seen on vehicles manufactured after October 1944. However, the gun mantlet on the ground in front of the vehicle pre-dates this, as does the 12-holed idler. A suspension unit, complete with part of the side armour, has been blown out. The area behind the missing mantlet is lighter in colour, being RAL 7028 Dunkelgelb. According to the diary of Helmus, 1./Pz.Jg.Abt.26 and Pz.Jg.Abt.1026 were in the Assenois – Sibret area between 22 and 24 December 1944. Note: The 1./Pz.Jg.Abt.26 was equipped with towed Pak 40s, while 2./Pz.Jg.Abt.26 was equipped with the Jagdpanzer 38. To confuse the enemy about the true nature of the 2nd Company, it was also designated Pz.Jg.Abt.1026. In theory, the Jagdpanzer should have had tactical numbers starting with '2'. The fighting for Sibret lasted from 25 to 27 December 1944.

2x Stefan De Meyer Collection

Another Jagdpanzer 38, minus its gun mantlet, is shown here backed into the shell of a farm building. Unlike the vehicle on the previous pages, it still has its roof. Its factory-applied 'disc' camouflage pattern is barely visible on the front plate, along with remnants of whitewash. Without a specific location, it is impossible to identify the unit.

Stefan De Meyer Collection

This Panzer IV/70(V) from 1./ or 2./Pz.Jg.Abt.3, 3.Panzergrenadier-Division, has ended its days in a stream in Chenogne, Belgium, unable to reverse out and with its gun embedded in the bank. Like many Jagdpanzers, visibility was poor; the driver had two periscopes: one for vision directly in front and the other angled 5° downwards. Therefore, the driver would have only have realised there was a ditch when the vehicle came to a shuddering halt. The cover for the loader's M.G.42 is open, revealing how much lighter the paint is underneath. This view also provides a rare glimpse of the roof.

Stefan De Meyer Collection

This Panzer IV/70(V) was photographed next to the customs building on the N15 north of Bohey, Luxembourg. It belonged to SS-Pz.Jg.Abt.1, 1.SS-Panzer-Division, attached to SS-Kampfgruppe Keil, and was destroyed on 12 January 1945 while attempting to reopen the Bastogne – Nothum road. The attack was supported by two Pz.IV/70(V). During the attack, the first vehicle tried to pass a destroyed Sherman, when it hit a mine and bogged down. The crew bailed out unharmed and withdrew together with the other vehicle to the rear, leaving the infantry without fire support. This ended the attack, and the Kampfgruppe withdrew in the evening. It has an AP scar on the side of the fighting compartment, but it is evident that something exploded near the front, destroying the travel lock and blowing off one of the vents on the brake access hatches.

1x NARA, 1x Stefan De Meyer Collection, 1x Panzerwrecks

The US 644th Tank Destroyer Battalion knocked out this Panzer IV/70(V) from SS-Pz. Jg.Abt.12 or s.H.Pz.Jg.Abt.560 in Domaine Bütgenbach on 18 December 1944. The vehicle is unusual in that it has a 'Rundumfeuer' M.G. mount fitted to the roof, which would not have been done at the factory. Although the photo is poor, we can see where a US 76mm anti-tank round went through the gun mount.

Panzerwrecks

A Sherman from the US 3rd Armored Division and a Panzer IV/70(V) from 8./SS-Pz.Rgt.2, 2.SS-Panzer-Division (tactical number '812'), side by side near Sterpigny; both were knocked out between 15 and 17 January 1945. The lower photo was taken in 1946 and shows that the Pz.IV/70's tracks are missing. Three tightly grouped holes in the side of the Sherman can also be seen.

From 15 to 18 January 1945, 12.Volksgrenadier-Division and elements of 2.SS-Panzer-Division were engaged in combat around Courtil, Baclain, Sterpigny, and Bovigny. By 15 January, the 12.VGD was significantly depleted, with only 250 Grenadiers remaining and no longer combat-ready. SS-Pz.Gren.Rgt.19 extended its defensive line from west of Courtil to Sterpigny, supported by I./SS-Pz.Rgt.9 and remnants of SS-Pz.Jg.Abt.9, now acting as infantry. SS-Pz.Pi.Btl.9 held the line between Courtil and Bovigny.

To compensate for heavy losses, the division redeployed supply units. SS-Pz.Gren.Rgt.4 withdrew to a new position along the Sterpigny-Cherain-Sommerain road. On the night of 15-16 January, orders arrived to withdraw the 12.Volks-Grenadier-Division for rest and refit.

On 16 January, intense fighting for Sterpigny resulted in heavy casualties on both sides. III./SS-Pz.Gren.Rgt.19 and I./SS-Pz.Rgt.9 endured the primary assault, with II./SS-Pz.Art.Rgt.9 and SS-Werf.Abt.502 also suffering due to delayed artillery position changes. The 2.SS-Panzer-Division consolidated its forces at Sommerain, repelling enemy advances with small groups from II./SS-Pz.Gren.Rgt.4 and limited tank support. Command and artillery positions were established east of Rettigny, and by nightfall, orders were given to withdraw SS-Pz.Gren.Rgt.4.

On 17 January, 'Hohenstaufen' began retreating eastward, with SS-Pz.Gren.Rgt.20 in the Courtil-Bovigny area and SS-Pz.Gren.Rgt.19 east of Sterpigny. I./SS-Pz.Gren.Rgt.19 stayed at Sterpigny with the 2.SS-Pz.Div. taking over a new defensive line in the woods east of Sterpigny. This line was held by remnants of SS-Pz.Pi.Btl.2, the division's assault company, SS-Pz.Rgt.2, and I./SS-Pz.Gren.Rgt.19, with artillery support from SS-Pz.Art.Rgt.2.

2x Stefan De Meyer Collection

A Sturmgeschütz IV from Stu.Gesch.Kp.1012, 12.Volksgrenadier-Division, photographed in Courtil, Belgium, in use as a signpost. In front of the loader's hatch is the mount for a Rundumfeuer M.G., although the mount looks to be blanked off, so it was probably not fitted at the factory. To enable a machine gun to be used, a post has been welded further forward; in front of the sliding gunsight guide. The tracks on the bow armour are the wider 'Winterketten' type, unlike all the other tracks on the vehicle.

2x Stefan De Meyer Collection

At the start of the Ardennes Offensive, 3.Fallschirmjäger-Division had no heavy armour. To remedy this, 1./Pz.Jg.Abt.348 was attached with 10 Sturmgeschütz IVs. The company lost six vehicles in the fighting between Thirimont and Amel, the last on 19 January during the defence of Eibertingen, 1 km west of Amel, as part of the III./Fsch.Jg.Rgt.9. According to men of the 3.Fsch.Jg.Div., the German tanks in Eibertingen managed to destroy a couple of American tanks at 'Am Kreuz' during their approach to Eibertingen and claimed that a single German assault gun, which had lost its tracks, held out until it fired its last round. Then the crew blew up the gun and withdrew. The Americans later identified this vehicle as a 75mm assault gun on a Mark IV chassis. The two other German tanks in the village had withdrawn in the meantime due to a lack of ammunition. **NARA**

This page and opposite: On 25 December 1944, this Sturmgeschütz III Ausf.G, from Fallschirm-Sturmgeschütz Brigade XI, was positioned between two houses in Sainlez, holding up the US 4th Armored Division tanks until it was destroyed by two 500lb bombs dropped by a P-47 Thunderbolt from the US 377th Fighter Squadron. Opposite: The three P-47 pilots who strafed and bombed in the immediate vicinity examined the wreckage. Left to right: Capt. Lowell K. Brueland, Capt. Francis P. McIntire, and 1st Lt. Loyd J. Overfield.

1x NARA, 2x Stefan De Meyer Collection

Tiger '008', commanded by Ustuf. Kalinowski, the adjutant of s.SS-Pz.Abt.501, was abandoned on 24 December 1944 between Trois Ponts and Stavelot, near the Ferme Antoine, the command post of Stubaf. Knittel. **Top left:** US engineers have rigged the Tiger to be pulled from the road. The tow cable around the gun barrel was used to turn the turret because the crew had set a demolition charge, which blew off the commander's hatch and probably destroyed the traverse mechanism. **Left and above:** The Tiger in its final resting place.

2x Stefan De Meyer Collection, 1x T.Haasler

Being on the side of the N23 to Stavelot, the Tiger was photographed quite a lot, and from a similar vantage point, as we see here. The factory-applied camouflage pattern is clearly visible on the glacis, with the large letter 'G' indicates that the tank has 'Glysantin' anti-freeze in its cooling system.

3x Stefan De Meyer Collection

Tiger in the grass. The gun looks shorter that usual because it is stuck at full recoil, possibly because the crew drained the recoil fluid or due to the internal explosion. The camouflage was applied at the Henschel factory before the trackguards were fitted.

Stefan De Meyer Collection

Being the adjutant's tank, Tiger '008' was a Befehlswagen (command vehicle), one of only 20 assembled. Externally, the differences were an armoured pot for an extra antenna on the engine deck, an extra antenna base on the turret roof behind the loader's hatch, and a tube carried at the junction of the rear plate and engine deck to stow the extra antennas.

Internally, ammunition stowage for the gun was reduced from 84 to 63 to make room for extra radios. The armoured pot can be seen here, as can the opened spent casing ejection port on the turret roof.

Stefan De Meyer Collection